THE PIG-TALE

THE
PIG-TALE

by

Lewis Carroll

Illustrated by

Leonard B. Lubin

Little, Brown and Company

Boston   *Toronto*

FIRST EDITION

T 04/75

"The Pig-Tale" is taken from *Sylvie and Bruno*
by Lewis Carroll, first published in 1889.

Some stanzas and selected drawings from this book appeared
prior to its publication in the April 1975 issue of *Cricket* Magazine.

Library of Congress Cataloging in Publication Data

Dodgson, Charles Lutwidge, 1832–1898. (Lewis Carroll)
    The pig-tale.

    [1.   Nonsense verses]   I.   Lubin, Leonard B., illus.
II.   Title.
PZ8.3.D667Pi5   821'.8   74–13424
ISBN 0–316–13006–0

*Published simultaneously in Canada
by Little, Brown & Company (Canada) Limited*

PRINTED IN THE UNITED STATES OF AMERICA

For Gerry and Lynda Hoover, with affection.

—L. L.

*L*ittle Birds are dining
   Warily and well,
    Hid in mossy cell:
   Hid, I say, by waiters
   Gorgeous in their gaiters—
    I've a Tale to tell.

Little Birds are feeding
   Justices with jam,
    Rich in frizzled ham:
   Rich, I say, in oysters
   Haunting shady cloisters—
    That is what I am.

Little Birds are teaching
Tigresses to smile,
Innocent of guile:
Smile, I say, not smirkle—
Mouth a semicircle,
That's the proper style.

Little Birds are sleeping
All among the pins,
Where the loser wins:
Where, I say, he sneezes
When and how he pleases—
So the Tale begins.

There was a Pig that sat alone
　　Beside a ruined Pump:
By day and night he made his moan—
It would have stirred a heart of stone
To see him wring his hoofs and groan,
　　Because he could not jump.

A certain Camel heard him shout—
   A Camel with a hump.
"Oh, is it Grief, or is it Gout?
What is this bellowing about?"
That Pig replied, with quivering snout,
   "Because I cannot jump!"

That Camel scanned him, dreamy-eyed.
   "Methinks you are too plump.
I never knew a Pig so wide—
That wobbled so from side to side—
Who could, however much he tried,
   Do such a thing as *jump!*

et mark those trees, two miles away,
All clustered in a clump:
If you could trot there twice a day,
Nor ever pause for rest or play,
In the far future—Who can say?—
  You may be fit to jump."

That Camel passed, and left him there,
  Beside the ruined Pump.
Oh, horrid was that Pig's despair!
His shrieks of anguish filled the air.
He wrung his hoofs, he rent his hair,
  Because he could not jump.

here was a Frog that wandered by—
  A sleek and shining lump:
Inspected him with fishy eye,
And said, "O Pig, what makes you cry?"
And bitter was that Pig's reply,
  "Because I cannot jump!"

That Frog he grinned a grin of glee,
  And hit his chest a thump.
"O Pig," he said, "be ruled by me,
And you shall see what you shall see.
This minute, for a trifling fee,
  I'll teach you how to jump!

"You may be faint from many a fall,
  And bruised by many a bump:
But, if you persevere through all,
And practice first on something small,
Concluding with a ten-foot wall,
  You'll find that you *can* jump!"

That Pig looked up with joyful start:
  "O Frog, you *are* a trump!
Your words have healed my inward smart—
Come, name your fee and do your part:
Bring comfort to a broken heart,
    By teaching me to jump!"

"My fee shall be a mutton-chop,
    My goal this ruined Pump.
Observe with what an airy flop
I plant myself upon the top!
Now bend your knees and take a hop,
    For that's the way to jump!"

Uprose that Pig, and rushed, full whack,
  Against the ruined Pump:
Rolled over like an empty sack,
And settled down upon his back,
While all his bones at once went "Crack!"
  It was a fatal jump.

*L*ittle Birds are writing
　　Interesting books,
　　　To be read by cooks:
Read, I say, not roasted—
Letterpress, when toasted,
　　Loses its good looks.

Little Birds are playing
　　Bagpipes on the shore,
　　　Where the tourists snore:
"Thanks!" they cry. " 'Tis thrilling!
Take, oh take this shilling!
　　Let us have no more!"

Little Birds are bathing
Crocodiles in cream,
Like a happy dream:
Like, but not so lasting—
Crocodiles, when fasting,
Are not all they seem!

That Camel passed, as Day grew dim
    Around the ruined Pump.
"O broken heart! O broken limb!
It needs," that Camel said to him,
"Something more fairy-like and slim,
    To execute a jump!"

That Pig lay still as any stone,
    And could not stir a stump:
Nor ever, if the truth were known,
Was he again observed to moan,
Nor ever wring his hoofs and groan,
    Because he could not jump.

That Frog made no remark, for he
    Was dismal as a dump:
He knew the consequence must be
That he would never get his fee—
And still he sits, in miserie,
    Upon that ruined Pump!

Little Birds are choking
Baronets with bun,
Taught to fire a gun:
Taught, I say, to splinter
Salmon in the winter—
Merely for the fun.

Little Birds are hiding
    Crimes in carpet-bags,
        Blessed by happy stags:
Blessed, I say, though beaten—
Since our friends are eaten
    When the memory flags.

Little Birds are tasting
    Gratitude and gold,
        Pale with sudden cold
Pale, I say, and wrinkled—
When the bells have tinkled,
    And the Tale is told.

R